LOVE IS
AND
LOVE
CAN BE

CHARLES LEE SMITH JR.

authorHOUSE®

AuthorHouse™
1663 Liberty Drive
Bloomington, IN 47403
www.authorhouse.com
Phone: 1 (800) 839-8640

Published by AuthorHouse   08/12/2016

ISBN: 978-1-5049-6645-0 (sc)
ISBN: 978-1-5049-6644-3 (e)

DEDICATION

THIS IS DEDICATED TO THE YOUNG
AND OLD, ELDERS OR ANYONE
WHO KNOWS THAT THEY'RE IN LOVE
WITH THEIR SIGNIFICANT OTHER,
AND LOVE BEING THERE, THOSE WHO
HAVE INVESTED TIME AND MONEY
AND SPACE, AND HAVE POURED OUT
THEIR SOUL TO THAT PERSON AND
HAVE REAPED FROM IT OR NOT, YOUR HEART
AND SOUL TOLD YOU, YOU WHERE IN LOVE.
THE BIBLE SAYS WHEN YOU PRAY TO GOD FOR
ANYTHING, DO NOT HAVE ANY DOUBT THAT YOU
WILL RECEIVE ANYTHING, BECAUSE DOUBTING
KILLS YOUR FAITH, IN MY PRAYERS I ASK THE
FATHER TO BLESS ME TO BLESS HIM AND
TO BLESS HIS CHILDREN, RIGHT AWAY MY GIFT
(BLESSING) IS FLOODED WITH THIS GREAT
ABILITY TO WRITE TO INSPIRE, SO THIS BOOK
IS ALSO DEDICATED TO THOSE I INSPIRE.
IN ADDITION TO THAT IM HOPING TO INSPIRE
OTHERS TO LET THEIR SIGNIFICANT OTHER
KNOW THAT THEY LOVE THEM, AND TO TAKE
MY POETRY IN CONCIDERATION TO PASS ON
TO THAT PERSON TO OPENLY EXPRESS THOSE
FEELINGS, I WOULD BE HONORED,
GIVING GLORY AND HONOR TO THE MOST
HIGH GOD OVER ALL IN MY LIFE

CHARLES LEE SMITH JR.

CONTENTS

DEDICATION v

WHAT IS LOVE 1
LOVE IS RIGHT HERE 2
THE ONLY ONE 3
THE LOVE OF YOU 4
MARRIAGE CAN BE 5
WHERE LOVE IS 6
DAYS END / LOVES DEN 7
YOUR HEARTS SPACE 8
WITH YOUR LOVE 9
EVERYTHING FOR OUR TEAM 10
HEART'S JOURNEY 11
EVERY NEW DAY 12
LOVE IS IN THE AIR 13
MATCHING HEARTS-A.. 14
HER SMILE SAYS A LOT..15
PARADISE FOR MY EYES ONLY 16
LUCKY ME 17
FEED ME-A 18
YOU'RE STILL-A..19
TEAM TODAY.. 20
ALL THE TIME 21
FEED ME –B 22
EVERYDAY WITH YOU.. 23
LIFE TIME OF LOVE* 24
FOOL IN LOVE 25
MATCHING HEARTS-B.. 26

THE THOUGHT OF YOU-A 27
HOW MY HEART KNOWS 28
THE ONLY MAN I LOVE 29
ME AND DAD 30
JUST LIKE YOU 31
THANKING YOU 32
MADE YOU TO BE 33
I CAN SAY 34
MY FIRST EVERYTHING... 35
GOD CHOOSES.. 36
A SPECIAL KIND 37
MY WIFE... 38
LET IT DO 39
MY FAVORITE DREAM... 40
KEEPING HER 41
LOVES CONNECT.. 42
FIRST PEEK 43
YOU'RE STILL-B.. 44
THE THOUGHT OF YOU-B 45
LOVE IS.. 46
OF YOU/ALWAYS DREAMING 47
MARRIAGE/WE ARE ONE 48
SANDBOX LOVE 49
WHO WOULD'VE KNOWN....................................... 50
NOW IT'S JUST YOU AND ME 51
CHOCOLATE FLOWER 52
THOSE HAZEL EYES.. 53
MEN LOVE YOUR WIVES 54
LOST IN YOUR EYES... 55
TWO HEARTS TOGETHER 56

ABOUT THE AUTHOR 57

WHAT IS LOVE

WHAT IS LOVE
WITHOUT A HEART
AND WHAT IS A HEART FOR
IF IT CAN'T LOVE
LET LOVE GENERATE
YOUR HEART
THEN LET YOUR HEART
GENERATE LOVE
BECAUSE LOVE IS JOY
LOVE BRINGS PEACE
LOVE CAN BE BEAUTIFUL
LOVE CAN BE SWEET
LOVE CAN BE A LIFETIME
LOVE CAN SET YOU FREE
THAT'S THE LIFE
FOR YOU AND ME

-BY CHARLES LEE SMITH JR.

LOVE IS RIGHT HERE

LOVE HAS BEEN RIGHT HERE
READY TO LOVE YOU
WANTING TO LOVE YOU
NEEDING YOUR LOVE
BECAUSE I LOVE, YOUR LOVE
YOUR LOVE IS BEAUTIFUL, WONDERFUL
AND MY LOVE, HAS BEEN RIGHT HERE
WAITING ON YOUR LOVE
SO LET YOUR LOVE GO
SO THAT OUR LOVE CAN GROW
TO BECOME ONE
TO BE COMPLETE
TO BECOME UNCONDITIONAL

- BY CHARLES LEE SMITH JR.

THE ONLY ONE

TRULY I HAVE FAVOR ON ME
TO WAKE UP EVERYDAY
WITH AN ANGEL
NEXT TO ME
DIVINE INTERVENTION
IS WHAT I WILL CALL THIS
BECAUSE THIS BEAUTY
I ONLY GET TO SEE
TO KEEP
HOW BLESSED AM I
I HAVE THE ONLY ONE OF HER KIND
I KNOW!!
IM HONORED BY THE MOST HIGH

-BY CHARLES LEE SMITH JR.

THE LOVE OF YOU

IF I WAS LOST AND LOST IT ALL
MEMORY GONE
YOUR LOVE WOULD BRING ME
BACK TO YOU
RESTORE IT ALL
BECAUSE THAT WOULD BE THE THING
THAT MY HEART WOULD HOLD TRUE
THE LOVE OF YOU
THE SMELL THE TOUCH OF YOU
BECAUSE MY LOVE IS YOU
'YES' YOU ARE MY LOVE
LIKE A DOVE COMING FROM ABOVE
A SHINING LIGHT SHINING BRIGHT
GIVING MY HEART SIGHT
TO FIND THOSE BEAUTIFUL FEELINGS
THAT MY HEART HOLDS TRUE
THE LOVE OF YOU

-BY CHARLES LEE SMITH JR.

MARRIAGE CAN BE

IN MY DREAMS YOU HAVE A PLACE
AND IN MY HEART YOU OCCUPY SPACE
BECAUSE THE ENERGY YOU DRAW
CAN'T BE REPLACED
YOUR KISS YOUR TOUCH, YOUR IRRESISTABLLE LOVE
NOT ANOTHER DAY DO I WANT
TO LIVE WITHOUT IT
WHEN I GO TO SLEEP I WANT YOU THERE
WHEN I WAKE UP
I NEED YOU IN MY ATMOSPHERE
ME, YOU AND GOD MAKES IT CLEAR
MARRIAGE IS WHAT IT'S CALLED
LIFE TOGETHER YEAR AFTER YEAR
LIFE TOGETHER WITHOUT FEAR
YES WE ARE ONE ALL COMPLETE AND WHOLE
LOCKED AT OUR HEARTS AND OUR SOULS
WE WILL ENDEAVER LIFE
WITH UNCONDITIONAL LOVE
LIVING OUT GOD'S DIVINE PLAN
FOR WOMAN AND MAN

-BY CHARLES LEE SMITH JR.

WHERE LOVE IS

LOVE IS
THE FIRST TIME MY EYES SAW YOU
WAS THE FIRST TIME MY HEART SAID
"I DO"
MY SOUL FOLLOWED
AND SOON AFTER MY BODY TOO
THE SMILE ON MY FACE
LASTED FOR DAYS
ON YOUR BEAUTY AND YOUR GRACE
MY MIND WAS STUCK IN A DAZE
BECAUSE THE WAY YOU MOVE WAS
BEAUTIFUL AND SMOOTH LIKE
THE SKIN ON YOUR FACE
YOUR VOICE …
MUSIC TO MY EARS
"YES" THIS IS WHERE LOVE IS
THIS IS WHERE I'LL BE, WITH YOU MY LOVE

-BY CHARLES LEE SMITH JR.

DAYS END / LOVES DEN

DAYS LIKE THIS MAKE ME WANT TO
LAY IT DOWN AND QUIT
DAYS LIKE THIS MAKE ME WANT TO BEAT
THE WORLD WITH A STICK
MAKES ME WANT TO BE A MAGICIAN
SO I CAN CHANGE THE WORLD
WITH A MAGIC TRICK
BECAUSE MY JOB IS ALMOST LIKE A DRUG FIX
BUT THEN I STEP BACK AND TAKE A MINUTE TO
MYSELF, AND IN THAT MINUTE I BECOME STEALTH
MY HEART STARTS RACING AND POUNDING
MY MIND GOES BLANK, BUT THEN A NEW PICTURE
SURROUNDS IT, AND JUST FOR A FEW MINUTES
IM REMINDED OF MY BEST FRIEND, MY WIFE,
AND MY KIDS, AND HOW MUCH FUN IT IS
IN MY DAYS END
YEP THAT'S WHERE LOVE IS, AND I CAN'T
WAIT TO GET HOME AGAIN
TO BE IN MY LOVES DEN

-BY CHARLES LEE SMITH JR.

YOUR HEARTS SPACE

IT'S CRAZY HOW I CAN BE
SO ANGRY
AND MY ANGER SOMETIMES
TURNS INTO RAGE
BUT SOON AS I SEE
YOUR FACE
IMMEDIATELY I'M IN YOUR HEARTS SPACE
A PLACE OF PEACE
A PLACE WHERE MY HEART SPEAKS
AND MY HEART IS SAYING
WHY CAN'T I STAY HERE
WHERE LIFE SEEMS SO SWEET
LEAVE ME HERE
AND THROW AWAY THE KEY

-BY CHARLES LEE SMITH JR.

WITH YOUR LOVE

IT IS HERE WITH
YOUR LOVE
I'M ABLE TO LET GO OF MY FEARS
HERE WITH YOUR LOVE
I CAN ESTABLISH THE YEARS
WITH YOUR LOVE THERES
A SPECIAL ATMOSPHERE
IT IS HERE WHERE I WILL
LET MY LOVE GO
TO GROW TO FLOW TO EXPERIENCE
LOVES BEAUTIFUL

-BY CHARLES LEE SMITH JR

EVERYTHING FOR OUR TEAM

TOGETHER WE ARE TEAM
REVERENCING WHAT LOVE IS
BECAUSE FOR OUR TEAM
LOVE IS EVERYTHING
AS A TEAM, AND THROUGH IT
WE'VE HAD OUR BEST BLESSING
NEVER HAVING TO BE ALONE
HAVING EACH OTHER TO BE STRONG
HAVING OUR CHILDREN
"YES" THEY WILL CARRY US ON
BECAUSE THROUGH THEM
WE SEE THE WORK WE PUT IN
WE SEE GOD'S DIVINE PLAN
FOR WOMAN AND MAN

-BY CHARLES LEE SMITH JR.

HEART'S JOURNEY

A HEART ON A LONG JOURNEY
LOOKING FOR THAT HEART
THAT HAS THE KEYS
TO UNLOCK ITS DOORS
MAKING LOVE TO "ALL OF YOU "
IS LIKE FINDING A TREASURE
WHAT A JOURNEY WHAT A PLEASURE
TO FIND TREASURE
EVERYTIME MY LIPS MEET YOURS
EVERYTIME YOUR HEART OPENS ITS DOORS
WHAT AN ASSORTMENT OF JEWELS TO BE HELD

YOUR FAITHFULNESS YOUR PASSION JUST FOR ME
YOUR UNCONDITIONAL LOVE
THOSE ARE THE HIDDEN TREASURES OF LOVE
AND A MAN WILL SEARCH THE ENDS OF THE WORLD
ONLY TO FIND THOSE TREASURES
CAN ONLY COME FROM ABOVE
PLACED INSIDE OF YOU TO COMPLETE OUR LOVE
TO BE ONE TO BE WHOLE
TO BE LOVED

-BY CHARLES LEE SMITH JR.

EVERY NEW DAY

EVERY NEW DAY
GIVES ME A NEW CHANCE
AND A NEW WAY
TO SAY
I LOVE YOU,
A NEW FIRST KISS
AND A NEW HUG
AND BECAUSE IT'S A NEW DAY
IT'S BRAND NEW LOVE

-BY CHARLES LEE SMITH JR.

LOVE IS IN THE AIR

AS LONG AS WE'RE TOGETHER
LOVE IS IN THE AIR
DOESN'T MATTER THE WEATHER
AS LONG AS YOU AND I ARE THERE
HOLDING HANDS OR HUGGED UP CLOSE
I NEED YOU IN MY ATMOSPHERE
AND THAT'S THE THING I LOVE MOST
BECAUSE WHEN WE ARE TOGETHER
WE ARE ONE
"YES" WHEN WE ARE TOGETHER
I FEEL COMPLETE AND WHOLE
BECAUSE WHEN YOUR LIPS MEET MINE
IT TOUCHES MY SOUL
AND WHEN WE ARE TOGETHER
I FEEL IT ALL IN THE AIR
LOVE IS EVERYWHERE

-BY CHARLES LEE SMITH JR.

MATCHING HEARTS-A

IF YOU'RE LOOKING FOR LOVE
AND YOU'RE LOOKING IN THE RIGHT PLACES
IT WILL BE YOUR HEART
THAT WILL MATCH ITS OWN FACE
SO LISTEN TO YOUR HEART
AND HAVE PATIENCE
NOW LOOK AT THE ONE
IN FRONT OF YOU
AND IF THAT HEART
MATCHES YOUR HEART'S FACE
THEN TODAY YOUR HEARTS LOVE
IS IN THE RIGHT PLACE

-BY CHARLES LEE SMITH JR.

HER SMILE SAYS A LOT

IF SHE'S CLEANING AND COOKING
WITH A SMILE ON HER FACE
AND MAKING SURE YOUR UNDERWARE ARE
FOLDED AND PUT AWAY, THAT'S WHERE LOVE IS
IF SHE BARES YOUR CHILDREN AND STILL MAINTAINS
HER GARDEN EVERYDAY, AND WHEN
FAMILY AND FRIENDS
COME AROUND AND THAT SAME
SMILE STUCK ON HER FACE
YOU BEST BELIEVE LOVE IS THERE
AND IT WILL PROBLY BE THERE FOR
THE REST OF YOUR DAYS
IF SHE KEEPS HER BODY UP
HER BUTT FIRM AND SOFT LIKE A POUND CAKE
HER BREAST STILL LIFTED AND FULL
LIKE THE FRUIT YOU LIKE MOST
FIRM AND RIPE
"YEAH" YOU GOT A MEAL FOR A LIFE TIME
SO YOU BEST STAND UP AND TREAT HER RIGHT
BECAUSE IT SOUNDS LIKE YOU GOT
LOVE FOR LIFE

-BY CHARLES LEE SMITH JR.

PARADISE FOR MY EYES ONLY

THROUGH MY EYES MY HEART SEES
THE BEAUTY IT DESIRES
A BEAUTY THAT'S MADE FOR ME
A BEAUTY THAT EVERYDAY
MY EYES OPEN
THEY WANT TO SEE
AN ISLAND ONLY I CAN TOUR
AN ISLAND JUST FOR ME TO EXPLORE
HOW BEAUTIFUL IT IS ON HER BEACH
MOST DAYS AND EVERYNIGHT
IS WHERE YOU WILL FIND ME
BECAUSE THE MOISTURE THAT RUNS
THROUGH HER SANDS
IS ALWAYS SWEET TO ME
MY OWN PARADISE ISLAND
JUST FOR ME

-BY CHARLES LEE SMITH JR.

LUCKY ME

ALTHO IM FULLY AWAKE
DARKNESS SURROUNDS ME
IN EVERY ASPECT PITCH BLACK IS ASTOUNDING
I CAN HEAR THE VOICES OF THE PEOPLE
I CAN HEAR THE SOUNDS OF STILETTOS
AND FLAT BOTTOM SHOES AS THEY ECHO THROUGH
AT THE SAME TIME IM ABLE TO NAVIGATE THROUGH
THEN SUDDENLY IT'S AS IF MY EYES ARE
OPENED FOR THE FIRST TIME
THIS LIGHT I SEE BLAZING DIRECTLY TOWARDS ME
AND AS IT COMES CLOSER HOW FINE HOW DIVINE
HOW BEAUTIFUL TO MY EYES
NOW SOMETHING HAS COME OVER ME
IM REMINDED OF MY DREAMS
"YEP" SHES THE WOMAN FROM MY DREAMS
MY WIFE RETURNING HOME TO ME
AND I GET THE SAME BLESSING EVERYDAY
EVERY SINCE WE EXCHANGED RINGS
"LUCKY ME"

-BY CHARLES LEE SMIYH JR.

FEED ME-A

IM A FOOL FOR YOU BABY
I'LL DO ANYTHING FOR YOU
IM A FOOL FOR YOU BABY
I GO ANYWHERE YOU
WANT ME TO
IM A FOOL FOR YOU BABY
JUST BECAUSE ITS YOU
FROM THE TOP OF YOUR HEAD
DOWN TO YOUR FEET
BECAUSE EVERYTHING ON YOUR
BODY LOOKS GOOD ENOUGH
TO EAT
A MEAL FOR A LIFETIME
MY SWEET TASTING VALENTINES
HAPPY VALENTINES

-BY CHARLES LEE SMITH JR.

YOU'RE STILL-A

UPS AND DOWNS
HEART BREAKS AND BREAK DOWNS
MISHAPPS AND TURN AROUNDS
LOVE ABUSED AND TRUST MISPLACED
BUT I KNOW YOUR HEART
IS THE ONLY ONE THAT MATCHES
MY HEARTS FACE
AND AFTER ALL THIS TIME
AND ALL WE'VE GONE THROUGH
YOU'RE STILL
MY VALENTINES

-BY CHARLES LEE SMITH JR.

TEAM TODAY

TEAM ALWAYS

TEAM LIFE TIME

TEAM US

TEAM YOU AND ME

TEAM VALENTINES

-BY CHARLES LEE SMITH JR.

ALL THE TIME

ALL THE TIME IS FOR
THE REST OF MY LIFE
AND FOR THE REST OF MY LIFE
I WANT YOU TO BE MY WIFE
MY BEST FRIEND
AND IF AT THE END
YOU'RE STILL MY BEST FRIEND
THEN ALL THE TIME
YOU WILL HAVE BEEN
MY VALENTINE

-BY CHARLES LEE SMITH JR.

FEED ME -B

IM A FOOL FOR YOU BABY
I'LL DO ANYTHING FOR YOU
IM FOOL FOR YOU BABY
I'LL GO ANYWHERE YOU
WANT ME TO
IM A FOOL FOR YOU BABY
JUST BECAUSE IT'S YOU
FROM THE TOP OF YOUR HEAD
DOWN TO YOUR FEET
BECAUSE EVERYTHING ON YOUR
BODY LOOKS GOOD ENOUGH
TO EAT
A MEAL FOR A LIFE TIME
YOU'RE THAT SWEET TASTING
LOVE OF MINE

-BY CHARLES LEE SMITH JR.

EVERYDAY WITH YOU

EVEN IF TODAY WASN'T VALENTINES
FOR YOU, WITH YOU
I WANT EVERYDAY TO BE VALENTINES
BECAUSE YOUR SPIRIT SPEAKS TO MINE
AND YOUR SMILE CAUSES MINE
YES YOUR HEARTS FACE
MATCHES MINE
NOW MY HEART KNOWS THAT
AFTER YOU, THERE COULD BE
NO OTHER VALENTINES IN MY LIFE
THIS IS WHY THIS DAY
I'M ASKING YOU TO BE
MY WIFE
MY VALENTINE FOR LIFE

-BY CHARLES LEE SMITH JR.

LIFE TIME OF LOVE

A VALENTINES FOOL
IS A FOOL THAT'S IN LOVE
A VALENTINES FOOL GOES
ABOVE AND BEYOND
IF YOU GOT A VALENTINES FOOL
THEN YOU GOT LOVE FOR A LIFE TIME
SINCE YOU GOT LOVE FOR
A LIFE TIME
THEN THAT MEANS
YOU WILL ALWAYS BE
MY VALENTINES

-BY CHARLES LEE SMITH JR.

FOOL IN LOVE

VALENTINES, DOES THAT MEAN
THAT YOU'RE MINE
FOR ALWAYS FOR ALL THE TIME
EVERYDAY IN EVERY WAY
DOES THAT MEAN
WHEN YOU SAY I LOVE YOU
THAT IT'S THE TRUTH
AND THAT IM NOT A FOOL
BUT I AM A FOOL FOR YOU BABY
AND IT'S THIS DAY AND THESE TIMES
AND FOR ALWAYS YOU'RE
MY VALENTINES

-BY CHARLES LEE SMITH JR.

MATCHING HEARTS-B

IF YOU'RE LOOKING FOR LOVE
AND YOU'RE LOOKING IN THE RIGHT PLACES
IT WILL BE YOUR HEART
THAT WILL MATCH ITS OWN FACE
SO LISTEN TO YOUR HEART
AND HAVE PATIENCE
NOW LOK AT THE ONE
IN FRONT OF YOU
AND IF THAT HEART
MATCHES YOUR HEART'S FACE
THEN TODAY YOUR VALENTINE'S
IN THE RIGHT PLACE
HAPPY VALENTINES DAY!!

-BY CHARLES LEE SMITH JR.

THE THOUGHT OF YOU-A

THE THOUGHT OF YOU
GIVES ME FEELINGS OF
COMPLETION AND WHOLENESS
THE THOUGHT OF YOU
CAUSES MY INNER MAN TO
STEP OUT IN A KINGS BOLDNESS
AND MY HEART KNOWING THIS
MY HEART IS LOOKING FOR
THE FIRST KISS OF MANY
LOOKING FOR A LIFE TIME OF PLENTY
PLENTY OF YOU, PLENTY OF US
WILL YOU BE MY WIFE
WILL YOU SHARE MY LIFE
SO THAT IT CAN BE
PLENTY OF YOU AND ME
AND YOU BEING MY FAVORITE DREAM

-BY CHARLES LEE SMITH JR.

HOW MY HEART KNOWS

THIS DAY IS A SPECIAL DAY
A DAY WHEN MY HEART PLAYS
A DAY WHEN MY HEART SPEAKS
AND MY HEART IS SAYING
IT HAS TO FIND THAT PLACE
WHERE IT CAN SHINE ALL DAY
THAT PLACE WHERE MY HEART
MATCHES ITS OWN FACE
AND THAT'S HOW
MY HEART KNOWS ITS
VALENTINES DAY

-BY CHARLES LEE SMITH JR.

THE ONLY MAN I LOVE

THE FIRST AND ONLY MAN
I FELL IN LOVE WITH
THE FIRST TIME I SAW
THE IMAGE OF GOD
THE ONE WHO SHOWED ME
HOW A MAN IS SUPPOSE TO
WORK HARD
AND HOW TAKING CARE OF HIS FAMILY
IS HIS JOB
MADE ME BELIEVE I WAS A CHIP
OFF THE OLD BLOCK
WHENEVER YOU CALLED ME SON
AND HOW WHEN MOM WOULD SAY
YOU'RE YOUR DADDIES SON
AND THAT'S THE THING THAT
ALWAYS MADE ME GLAD
KNOWING "YOU" WAS
MY DAD

-BY CHARLES LEE SMITH JR.

ME AND DAD

I REMEMBER THOSE DAYS
IN THE PARK
WITH A BAT BALL AND GLOVE
AND WHEN THE SEASONS CHANGED
FOOTBALL BECAME OUR NEXT LOVE
I KNOW WHAT I KNOW TODAY
BECAUSE YOU CHALLENGED ME TO LEARN
NOT JUST SPORTS, BUT
MY PAY CHECK HOW TO EARN
HARD WORK AND THE LOVE OF FAMILY
IS THE DREAM YOU INSTILLED IN ME
AND HOW THAT DREAM
AND RELATIONSHIP WITH GOD
SHOULD BE THE THING THAT
MOTIVATES ME
THANKS FOR BEING A PERFECT EXAMPLE
AND A MAN OF GOD
LOVE YOU DAD!!

-BY CHARLES LEE SMITH JR.

JUST LIKE YOU

DAD AND SON
TWO WORDS THAT FIT
LIKE A HAND IN A GLOVE
BECAUSE EVERYTHING
YOU SHOWED ME
YOU DID IT OUT OF LOVE
AND NOW IT'S MY TURN
BECAUSE NOW IM A DAD
AND I HAVE A SON
NOW I KNOW IT'S MY JOB
AND IT'S FOR HIM TO LEARN
SO THAT HE CAN CARRY
OUR TRADITIONS ON
AND I JUST WANTED TO SAY
THANKS DAD
FOR PREPARING ME FOR MY JOB
AND BEING WHO YOU ARE
MY FIRST BEST FRIEND
LOVE YOU DAD

-BY CHARLES LEE SMITH JR.

THANKING YOU

THANKS DAD
I CAN NEVER SAY IT ENOUGH
AND EVEN ON THIS SPECIAL DAY
IT WON'T BE SAID ENOUGH
BUT I'LL SAY IT ALL DAY
AND ON YOUR SPECIAL DAY
IM TRYING TO SAY IT
IN A VERY SPECIAL WAY
"THANKS DAD"
YOU'RE MY HERO
LOVE YOU ALWAYS

-BY CHARLES LEE SMITH JR.

MADE YOU TO BE

INSIDE OF YOU
GOD SHAPED AND
MOLDED ME
ALL INSIDE OF NINE MONTHS
HE PUT IN ME
WHO IM SUPPOSE TO BE
AND HE BLESSED YOU TOO
BECAUSE HE MADE YOU TO BE
A GREAT MOM FOR ME

-BY CHARLES LEE SMITH JR.

I CAN SAY

I CAN NEVER
REPAY YOU FOR
ALL YOU'VE DONE
BUT I CAN SAY
"I LOVE YOU"
MOM !!!

-BY CHARLES LEE SMITH JR.

MY FIRST EVERYTHING

THE FIRST TIME
I SAW LIFE
I SAW YOU
THE FIRST TIME
I EXPERIENCED LOVE
IT WAS YOURS
YOU HELD ME IN YOUR ARMS
THEN YOU SMOTHERED ME
WITH YOUR KISSES AND HUGS
RIGHT AWAY I RECEIVED
UNCONDITIONAL LOVE
A MOTHERS TYPE
LOVE THAT'S NICE
RIGHT FOR LIFE

-BY CHARLES LEE SMITH JR.

GOD CHOOSES

YOU DIDN'T CHOOSE ME
AND I DIDN'T CHOOSE YOU
GOD DID IT
HE CHOSE YOU FOR ME
AND ME FOR YOU
AND THAT'S WHY YOU ARE
WHO YOU ARE
MY LOVING MOM

-BY CHARLES LEE SMITH JR.

A SPECIAL KIND

THERE'S NO OTHER WOMAN
THAT'S MORE SPECIAL THAN YOU
BECAUSE THE MOM THAT YOU ARE
IS JUST SPECIAL PROOF
NOW EVERYONE WHO READS THIS
WILL KNOW IT TOO
THEY'LL SEE YOU AND THEY'LL
KNOW YOU'RE SPECIAL TOO
AND THAT TODAY, WAS MADE SPECIAL
JUST FOR YOU
I LOVE MOM

-BY CHARLES LEE SMITH JR.

MY WIFE

EVERYDAY
I SEE OUR KIDS
IS EVERYDAY
I GET TO SEE
HOW SPECIAL
THIS DAY IS
TO THE BEST WIFE
AND THE BEST MOM
MY BEST FRIEND
HAPPY MOTHERS DAY

-BY CHARLES LEE SMITH JR.

LET IT DO

THIS CARD IS NOT FOR PROOF
BUT TODAY
LET IT DO
WHAT IT SUPPOSE TO DO
SIMPLY TO SAY
"I LOVE YOU"

-BY CHARLES LEE SMITH JR.

MY FAVORITE DREAM

I WAS HAVING MY FAVORITE DREAM
THEN I WOKE UP
AND IT'S BEEN A NIGHTMARE SINCE
BECAUSE I WANT TO BE
IN THAT DREAM AGAIN " YEAH "
BE APART OF THAT SCENE AGAIN
MAKING LOVE TO YOU
MY FAVORITE DREAM

-BY CHARLES LEE SMITH JR.

KEEPING HER

WALKING WITH MY WIFE
IS WHERE I'LL BE
ON A JOURNEY OF LOVE
KEEPING HER HAPPY
I'LL BE WORKING HARD
AND IT WILL BE MY JOB
TO KEEP HER HONEST BEFORE GOD
AND EVERYDAY IM BLESSED TO SEE
IS EVERYDAY SHE'LL BE WITH ME
AND EVERYDAY
SHE WILL HEAR ME SAY
IN A SPECIAL WAY
"I LOVE YOU"

-BY CHARLES LEE SMITH JR.

LOVES CONNECT

DAY OR NIGHT
THE LORDS LOVE IS THERE
THROUGH HIS LIGHT
SHINING BRIGHT ON OUR HEARTS
OUR LOVE CONNECTED
FROM OUR EYES TO OUR HEART
FROM OUR HEART TO DEEP IN OUR SOUL
THE CONNECT WAS MADE WHOLE
AND OUR LOVE BECAME STRONG
AND EVERYDAY OUR LOVE
ENDURES THE TEST TO MAINTAIN IT'S BEST
AND AT NIGHT
WE SHARE IN LOVES REST
LOVES LIGHT LOVES CONNECT

-BY CHARLES LEE SMITH JR.

FIRST PEEK

WHEN MY EYES TAKE
THE FIRST PEEK OF THE DAY
I LOOK OVER YOUR WAY
MY SPIRIT STARTS TO FLY
NOW JOY IS IN MY EYES
BECAUSE I SEE A RARE BEAUTY LYING
BESIDES ME WITH UNCONDITIONAL LOVE
A TRUE BLESSING,
IT HAD TO COME FROM ABOVE
NOW THAT'S LOVE
TO BE BLESSED WITH LOVE

-BY CHARLES LEE SMITH JR.

YOU'RE STILL-B

UPS AND DOWNS
HEART BREAKS AND BREAK DOWNS
MISHAPPS AND TURN AROUNDS
LOVE ABUSED AND TRUST MISPLACED
BUT I KNOW YOUR HEART
IS THE ONLY ONE THAT MATCHES
MY HEARTS FACE
AND AFTER ALL THIS TIME
AND ALL WE'VE GONE THROUGH
YOU'RE STILL
THE ONE MY HEART
HOLDS TRUE

-BY CHARLES LEE SMITH JR.

THE THOUGHT OF YOU-B

THE THOUGHT OF YOU
GIVES ME FEELINGS OF
COMPLETION AND WHOLENESS
THE THOUGHT OF YOU
CAUSES MY INNER MAN TO
STEP OUT IN A KINGS BOLDNESS
AND MY HEART KNOWING THIS
MY HEART IS LOOKING FOR
THE FIRST KISS OF MANY
LOOKING FOR A LIFE TIME OF PLENTY
PLENTY OF YOU, PLENTY OF US
WILL YOU BE MY WIFE
WILL YOU SHARE MY LIFE
SO THAT IT CAN BE
PLENTY OF TIMES OF YOU BEING
MY VALENTINES!!!

-BY CHARLES LEE SMITH JR.

LOVE IS

L LETTING GO OF YOURSELF TO COMMIT TO SOMEONE ELSE

O OVERCOMING ALL ADVERSITY AND DISPARE TO REMAIN COMMITED TO THE ONE WHO YOU BEGAN YOUR COMMITMENT TO

V VIRTUOUS HONEST, AND VICTORIOUS IN YOUR COMMITMENT

E ETERNAL EVERLASTING COMMITMENT, EAGER AND READY TO PLEASE THE ONE WHOM YOU ARE COMMITED TO

-BY CHARLES LEE SMITH JR.

OF YOU/ALWAYS DREAMING

GOOD MORNING MY LOVE
THINKING ABOUT YOU
GETS MY HEART GOING
AND MY THOUGHTS START FLOWING
WITH THOUGHTS THAT TELL
THE REST OF ME
WHY IT LOVES YOU, AND HOW IT
CRAVES TO BE WITH YOU
AND HOW WHEN YOUR LIPS
MEET MINE IT STOPS TIME
AND BRINGS A WONDERFUL
PEACE TO MY BEING
THAT SAME PEACE
I HAVE WHEN IM SLEEPING
I GUESS THAT'S WHY OF YOU
IM ALWAYS DREAMING
MY FAVORITE DREAM

-BY CHARLES LEE SMITH JR.

MARRIAGE/WE ARE ONE

OUR DAY
A DAY OF MANY DAYS
A DAY FOR YOU AND ME
A DAY THAT WE ARE PRAISED
A DAY THAT WE COMMIT TO CHANGE OUR WAYS
A DAY TO BE REMEMBERED
TO REMIND US WHERE WE COME FROM
A DAY WE SHOULD REMEMBER
TO PUSH US TOWARDS OUR FUTURE
YOU AND I TOGETHER THROUGH ANY KIND OF WEATHER
BOUND AT OUR HEARTS AND LOCKED AT OUR SOULS
NOW YOU AND I ARE ONE ALL COMPLETE AND WHOLE
NOW YOU ARE MY WIFE AND I, I AM YOUR HUSBAND
NOW WE TAKE THIS STEP
TO SHARE IN LIFES BLESSINGS
NOW WE TAKE THIS STEP
TO WALK IN MARRIAGE HEAVEN

-BY CHARLES LEE SMITH JR.

SANDBOX LOVE

YOU'VE BEEN A PART OF MY SOUL
SINCE THE FIRST TIME I SAW YOU
SANDBOX KIDS
HANDLING KINDERGARDEN BUSINESS
IN THE HEART OF THE SUMMER
NOT KNOWING ANYTHING ABOUT LOVE
BUT THERE WE WERE CLOSER THAN CLOSE
WAY CLOSER THAN MOST
AS WE GOT OLDER
THE MORE YOU STARTED TO KNOW ME
THE MORE I STARTED TO NOTICE YOU
YOUR BODY STARTED TO REVEAL THINGS
MY CONVERSATION BECAME MORE APPEALING
THEN IT HAPPENED, OUR BODIES MET
LIKE A KEY TO A LOCK, A HAND TO A GLOVE
"YES" WE MADE LOVE
RGHT FROM THE SANDBOX
TO OUR FIRST CLOSE ENCOUNTER
NOW IN MARRIAGE WE ARE BEST FRIENDS
EVERYWHERE WE GO
THERE WE ARE HAND IN HAND
THIS HAD TO BE A DIVINE PLAN

-BY CHARLES LEE SMITH JR.

WHO WOULD'VE KNOWN

WHO WOULD'VE KNOWN

YOU AND I WOULD BE STILL TOGETHER
STILL GRINDING STILL ENJOYING
THE GOOD AND THE BAD WEATHER
AFTER ALL THESE YEARS
STILL ENJOYING LIFE TOGETHER

WHO WOULD'VE KNOWN

CHILDHOOD FRIENDS GROWING OLDER
SHARING CHILDHOOD DREAMS TOGETHER
BUYING A HOUSE HAVING KIDS TOGETHER

WHO WOULD'VE KNOWN

50 YEARS TOGETHER
GRANDKIDS AND GREAT GRANDS TOGETHER
AND THAT OUR MARRIAGE
WAS GONE LAST FOREVER
SANDBOX KIDS STILL TOGETHER
WHO WOULD'VE KNOWN

-BY CHARLES LEE SMITH JR.

NOW
IT'S JUST YOU AND ME

YOU ARE THE FLOWER
THAT GOD HAS CHOSEN
TO BRING FORTH MY SEED
HOW BEAUTIFUL AND SPECIAL
YOU ARE TO ME
TO BE WITH A BEAUTIFUL WOMAN
SHARING AND BRINGING FORTH
LIFE WITH ME
WATCHING THEM GROW OLDER
WATCHING THEM BECOME
WHO GOD INTENDED THEM TO BE
NOW THEY ARE WHO THEY ARE
AND NOW IT'S JUST
YOU AND ME
WE'VE GROWN OLDER
NOW WE CAN LIVE LIFE IN THE SWEET
IN A SMALL GARDEN
JUST YOU AND ME

BY- CHARLES

CHOCOLATE FLOWER

WHEN IM WITH MY
CHOCOLATE FLOWER
EVERY HOUR IS SWEET
FROM YOUR HEAD
DOWN TO YOUR FEET
YOU'RE THE FINEST PIECE
OF CHOCOLATE
AND YOU'VE GOT THE
SWEETEST SWEETS
SPREADED ALL IN
THAT LOVELY GARDEN
YOU KEEP
SWEET CHOCOLATE FLOWER
JUST FOR ME

- BY CHARLES LEE SMITH JR.

THOSE HAZEL EYES

GREEN BASED
WITH SMALL TRACES OF BROWN
AND A TOUCH OF GOLD
BEAUTIFUL AND BOLD
MEZMORISING WITH A STRONG HOLD
MY SOUL YOU TOOK AND YOU DIDN'T
EVEN KNOW
THAT MY HEART WAS YOURS
AND THAT I WAS GONE
LOST IN MY DAY DREAMS
EVERYDAY IMAGINING ME AND YOU
DOING WHAT TWO PEOPLE
IN LOVE DO
AND THE REALALITY OF IT ALL
IS "I GOT YOU"
THEN - THOSE HAZEL EYES -
ARE MINE TOO!!

- BY CHARLES LEE SMITH JR.

MEN LOVE YOUR WIVES

I WANNA TO LOVE MY WIFE

THE WAY IT'S SUPPOSE TO BE
HER AND ME INTWINED IN ECSTACY
JUST LIKE A DREAM OUR BODIES
ROLLED SO SWEET

I WANNA LOVE MY WIFE

WALKS IN THE PARK
IN THE MORN AND EVE
TALKS ABOUT KIDS AND WHAT
THEIR NAMES WOULD BE
HER AND ME AND OUR DEEPEST DREAMS
LIVING LIFE THE WAY IT'S SUPPOSE TO BE
BLESSED WITH JOY AND A LIFE OF PEACE

I WANNA LOVE MY WIFE

-BY CHARLES LEE SMITH JR,

LOST IN YOUR EYES

WHEN IM IN MY HAPPY PLACE
IT'S ALWAYS
WHEN WE'RE FACE TO FACE
I GET LOST IN YOUR EYES
WHERE I SEE OUR LOVE
FLYING HIGH IN THE SKY
TWO HEARTS WITH WINGS
DOING UNIMAGINARY THINGS
AND THINGS DEVINE
YEAH! LOST IN YOUR EYES
IS WHERE MY HEART WANTS TO STAY
MY HEART TOLD ME
IT'S THE MOST FUN PLACE
HE'S EVER PLAYED

YEAH! LOST IN YOUR EYES IS
MY HAPPY PLACE

-BY CHARLES LEE SMITH JR.

TWO HEARTS TOGETHER

LOVE IS ALWAYS THE BLANKET
THAT KEEPS US WARM
LOVE GIVES US THE STRENGTH TO CONTINUE ON
MY HEART HAS FOUND THE HEART
THAT HAS THE KEYS TO UNLOCK ITS DOORS
A HEART THAT CAN MEND
THE OLD WOUNDS FROM BEFORE
ONE THAT REASSURES,
AND OUR HEARTS WILL ALWAYS BE BEST FRIENDS
CAUSE YOUR HEART IS MY HEARTS TWIN
TWO HEARTS TOGETHER
ALL THE WAY TO THE END

-BY CHARLES LEE SMITH JR.

ABOUT THE AUTHOR

MY NAME IS CHARLES LEE SMITH JR. I HAVE THREE
CHILDREN CHARLES ISAIAH SMITH III, SHAY SHAY
SHERRY LAVERN SMITH AND MALACHI SMITH. IM
THE SECOND OLDEST OF FIVE CHILDREN, THE
SECOND OLDEST GRANDCHILD OF MY MOMS
PARENTS, AND MY DADS OLDEST CHILD.

AS A CHILD I EXCELLED IN SPORTS, BASEBALL BEING
MY PRIMARY SPORT. I GREW UP ON THE SOUTHSIDE
CHICAGO IL WHERE I ATTENDED CORLISS HS 80-84. AS
A YOUNG MAN I WATCHED MY DAD WRITE DOWN THE
SONGS THAT HE ENJOYED SINGING, HEARD MY MOM
SING A LOT AROUND THE HOUSE, I GUESS THAT PLAYED
A MAJOR ROLL IN MY SKILL SET. LOVING TO SING AND
WRITE, FOR MANY YEARS I RAN FROM THIS GIFT. I DID
NOT EMBRACE IT BECAUSE I WANTED TO WRITE R&B
BUT EVERYTHING WOULD COME OUT SPIRITUAL. AS I
GOT OLDER IT BECAME MORE APPARENT THAT IF I WAS
GOING TO WRITE IT WOULD BE JUST THAT, SPIRITUAL
AND UP LIFTING LITERITURE. MY FIRST PIECE CAME
OUT WONDERFUL, MAINLY BECAUSE OTHERS LIKED IT.

AT THAT TIME IT RESINATED DEEP WITH IN ME, AND
THAT DAY LEAD TO TODAY! IN ADDITION TO THAT, IN
MY PRAYERS I ASK THE MOST HIGH GOD TO BLESS ME
TO BLESS HIM TO BLESS HIS CHILDREN, AND BECAUSE
OF THAT LOVE IS THE FOUNDATION OF EVERYTHING I
WRITE. TO LOVE MY HEAVENLY FATHER, TO LOVE MY

PARENTS, TO LOVE MY WOMAN AND MY SEED, I ONLY HOPE THAT THIS BOOK WHEN FOUND BY THE READERS IT HELPS IN THEIR QUEST FOR LOVE, THAT IT GOES FORTH AND DOES WHAT ITS SUPPOSE TO DO INSPIRE AND UPLIFT IN EVERY READER'S LIFE OR SITUATION.

MAY THE MOST HIGH GOD BLESS
ALL THOSE WHO LOVE HIM!!

-BY CHARLES LEE SMITH JR.